YOUR BRAIN

Understand It with Numbers

Melanie Waldron

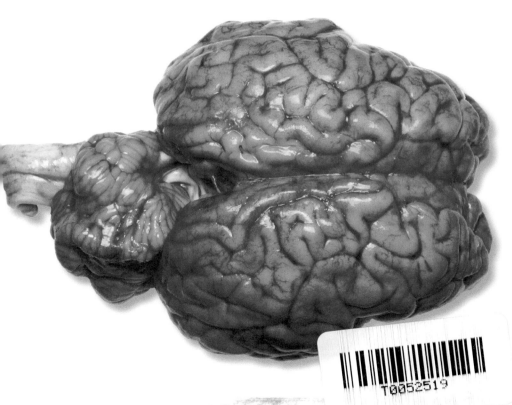

Chicago, Illinois

Produced for Raintree by
White-Thomson Publishing
www.wtpub.co.uk
+44 (0)843 208 7460

Edited by Sonya Newland
Designed by Tim Mayer
Original illustrations © Capstone 2014
Illustrated by HL Studios
Picture research by Sonya Newland Production
by Victoria Fitzgerald
Originated by Capstone Global Library Ltd

**Library of Congress Cataloging-in-Publication
Data**
Waldron, Melanie.
  Your brain : understand it with numbers /
Melanie Waldron.
    pages cm.—(Your body by numbers)
Includes bibliographical references and index.
ISBN 978-1-4109-5980-5 (hb)—ISBN
978-1-4109-5985-0 (pb) 1. Brain—Juvenile
literature. 2. Intellect—Juvenile literature. I.
Title.

  QP376.W22 2014
  612.8'2—dc23   2013016814

Acknowledgments
The author and publisher are grateful to
the following for permission to reproduce
copyright material:
Alamy p. 17 (Michael Doolittle); Capstone
Global Library p. 9; Dreamstime pp. 4
(Huaxiadragon), 5 left (Akhilesh), 7
(Sangiorzboy), 12 (Toa555), 21 (Cbpix),
22 (Cathykeifer), 24 (Orionmystery), 29 left
(Lukyslukys), 29 right (Oariff), 30 (Juemic),
31 (Monkeybusinessimages); Getty Images
p. 18 bottom (MedicalRF.com); Shutterstock
pp. 5 right (ollyy), 10 left (Sebastian Kaulitzki),
10 right (suravid), 11 (mast3r), 13 top (Leonello
Calvetti), 13 bottom (Rich Carey), 15 (Firma
V), 16 bottom (johannviloria), 23 bottom
(iodrakon), 25 bottom right (TTphoto), 26–27
top (Sebastian Kaulitzki), 26–27 bottom (Mark
Herreid), 28 top (Chepko Danil Vitalevich),
32 (panbazil), 33 (Goodluz), 34 top (Zurijeta),
37 (Debbie Steinhausser), 38 bottom (Ljupco
Smokovski), 39 (Monkey Business Images),
40 (Monkey Business Images), 42 (Marcio
Eugenio), 43 (Konstantin Shishkin); SuperStock
pp. 14 top (VEM/BSIP), 18 top (Jacopin/BSIP/
BSIP), 28 bottom (Radius), 35 (Eye Ubiquitous),
36 top (Garo/Phanie).

Cover photograph of brain anatomy (cross
section) reproduced with permission of
CLIPAREA/Custom media/Shutterstock.

Every effort has been made to contact copyright
holders of any material reproduced in this book.
Any omissions will be rectified in subsequent
printings if notice is given to the publisher.

All the Internet addresses (URLs) given in this
book were valid at the time of going to press.
However, due to the dynamic nature of the
Internet, some addresses may have changed, or
sites may have changed or ceased to exist since
publication. While the author and publisher
regret any inconvenience this may cause readers,
no responsibility for any such changes can be
accepted by either the author or the publisher.

CONTENTS

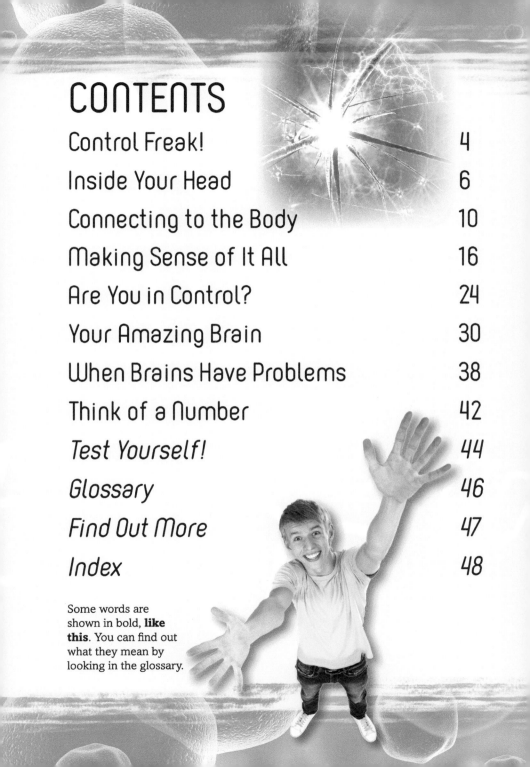

Some words are shown in bold, **like this**. You can find out what they mean by looking in the glossary.

Control Freak!

You probably think that you are in control of your body. After all, you (mostly) decide what you do and when you do it. But really it's your brain that is in control of you!

Gymnasts need to be strong and flexible, but they also need their brains to be in total control of their bodies.

Your brain is an amazing **organ** that sits in your head. It is what you use when you want parts of your body to move and carry out tasks. Your brain also runs all the body parts inside you and keeps them working together smoothly. You only have one brain to last your whole life. But count yourself lucky—some animals, such as starfish, don't have a brain at all!

High Fuel Consumption

Your brain's weight is about 2 percent of your total body weight. This might make you think that it only needs 2 percent of the energy you get from your food. But no! Your brain uses up a massive 20 percent of the energy you consume!

Storage Capacity

Do you have a computer? If so, what is its memory storage capacity? It might be 500 gigabytes, or a really flashy 1,000 gigabytes. But that's nothing compared to your brain. The brain has about 100,000 gigabytes worth of memory storage capacity!

100,000 GB

Think of a Number

In this book, we will look at lots of facts and figures about the brain. For starters, did you know that your brain is made of cells? These are the tiny building blocks that make up every part of your body. You have about 100 billion brain cells—that's about as many trees as there are in the Amazon rain forest. We will also look at what the brain is made of, how it works, and what it does.

Inside Your Head

Your brain weighs about 3 pounds (1.4 kilograms). Compare this to sperm whales—their brains weigh in at 17 pounds (7.8 kilograms)! However, sperm whales are a lot bigger than us—and body size is important...

Brain : Body Weight Ratio

When you think about the weight of an animal's brain, you also have to consider the total weight of the animal. You can then calculate a **ratio**. This gives you a figure showing how much bigger something is in relation to something else.

Let's consider the weight of a human brain compared to the weight of a human body. The body weighs about 40 times more than the brain. This gives a human brain : body weight ratio of 1 : 40.

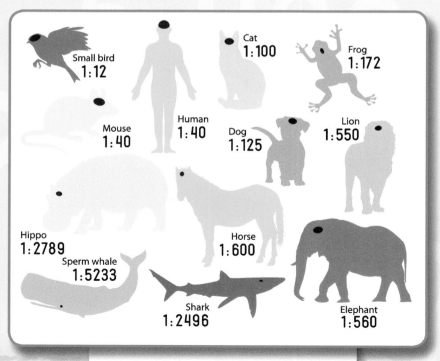

Small bird
1:12

Cat
1:100

Frog
1:172

Mouse
1:40

Human
1:40

Dog
1:125

Lion
1:550

Hippo
1:2789

Sperm whale
1:5233

Horse
1:600

Shark
1:2496

Elephant
1:560

This diagram shows the brain:body weight ratios for several animals.

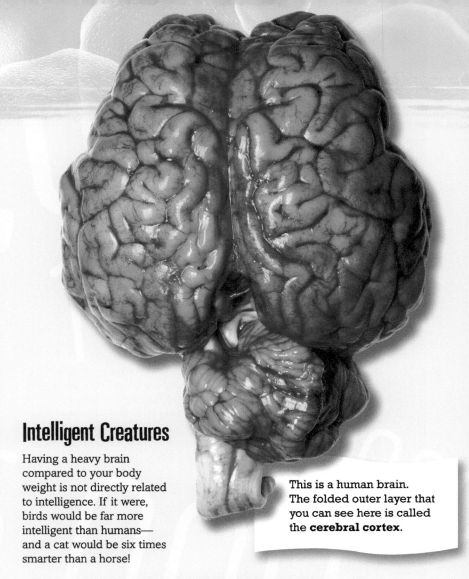

Intelligent Creatures

Having a heavy brain compared to your body weight is not directly related to intelligence. If it were, birds would be far more intelligent than humans— and a cat would be six times smarter than a horse!

This is a human brain. The folded outer layer that you can see here is called the **cerebral cortex**.

In fact, scientists think that intelligence relates more to the number of folds and grooves on the surface of the brain than its size. The human brain has lots of folds and grooves. If you smoothed out all the folds on the surface of a human brain and laid it flat, it would cover a big area. Having a large surface area means that the brain can store more information.

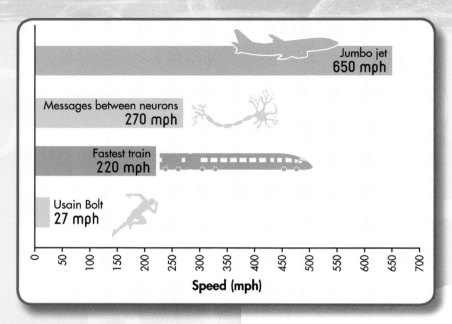

Jumbo jet 650 mph		
Messages between neurons 270 mph		
Fastest train 220 mph		
Usain Bolt 27 mph		

Speed (mph)

0 50 100 150 200 250 300 350 400 450 500 550 600 650 700

What Is It Made of?

Your brain is made of brain cells called **neurons**. They form a pinkish-gray gelatin-like dome, about the size of a small cauliflower. Your brain is about 75 percent water.

Your neurons can transmit messages up to 10 times faster than Usain Bolt—the fastest runner on Earth—can run! But a jumbo jet can go a lot faster. Some spy planes can go around four times as fast as a jumbo jet.

Neurons have spidery arms called **dendrites**. These connect to the **axons** —the long arms—of other neurons. Dendrites and axons carry electrical messages into and out of your brain. These connections are what keep your brain in control of your body. They are important not just for linking your brain to your body parts, but also for carrying out tasks such as storing your memories, figuring things out, and making decisions.

Brain Parts

The brain is made up of four main parts. Each part does different things. The cerebrum makes up almost 90 percent of your brain. It is covered in the folded cerebral cortex and is split into two halves—the left and right hemispheres. The cerebrum is where you do your thinking.

A Brain of Two Halves

The two cerebral hemispheres work on different things. The left brain deals with numbers, words, and finding solutions. The right brain deals with colors, sounds, shapes, music, and imagination. The two halves are connected by a bundle of fibers called the corpus callosum. Which side do you use most?

The cerebellum controls balance and movements. The diencephalon contains lots of parts that relate to feelings, senses, emotions, and body functions. The brain stem joins the brain to the rest of the body. It controls things such as your heartbeat and digestion.

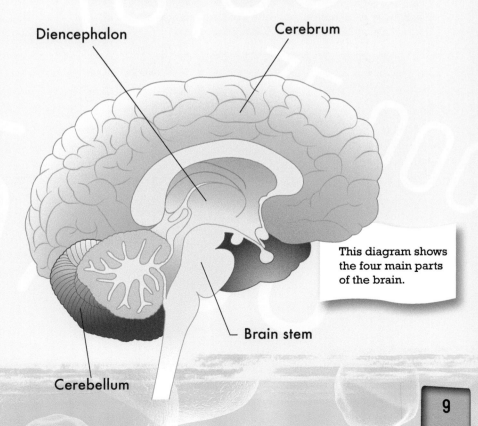

Diencephalon

Cerebrum

This diagram shows the four main parts of the brain.

Brain stem

Cerebellum

Connecting to the Body

Your brain sits on top of your body, but it controls all the different parts of it, right down to your little toe. Your body parts are connected to your brain by a huge network of nerve cells.

A World of Nerves

This network is your **nervous system**. Your spine contains the main bundle of **nerves**, called the spinal cord. All of the nerves that run to your legs, your arms, and the rest of your body branch out from the spinal cord. In total, there are around 93,000 miles (150,000 kilometers) of nerves in your body!

There are enough nerves in your body to stretch around Earth more than three times—the **circumference** of Earth is about 29,000 miles (40,000 kilometers).

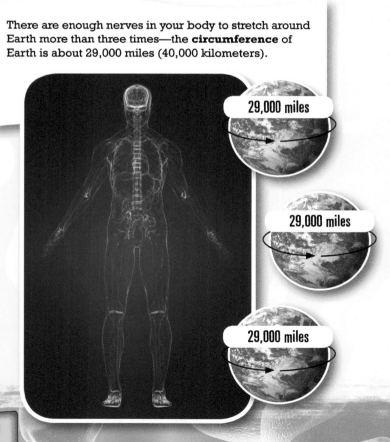

29,000 miles

29,000 miles

29,000 miles

Off/On, Fast/Slow

A nerve cell either sends a signal to the brain or it doesn't, just like a simple light switch is either on or off. So how can a signal, such as pain, seem strong or weak? It is all connected to the **frequency**—the number of signals sent every second. Mild pain sends far fewer signals to the brain every second than severe pain.

Width of sciatic nerve

Length of brain to eye nerves

Thickness of spinal cord

Long and Short

The nerves in the nervous system are different lengths and thicknesses. The thickest nerve is the **sciatic nerve**. This is in your upper leg and is about as wide as your thumb. The spinal cord is around the same thickness as your little finger. The nerves that connect your brain to your eyes are about the length of your thumb. The nerves going from the spinal cord to the toes are about 4 feet (1.2 meters) long.

Cord Comparisons

The spinal cord in a human is about 18 inches (45 centimeters) long. Compare this to a giraffe's spinal cord, which can be up to 8½ feet (2.6 meters) long!

Electric Shocks

The signals sent through your nervous system, connecting your body to your brain, are electrical signals. But they are not like the electricity that travels through wires to power your gadgets. Electrical signals in the body jump from one nerve cell to the next, all the way from the brain to the body part, and vice versa. Each signal is about 0.1 volts of electricity. This is quite small—you would need a 1.5 volt battery to power a small flashlight.

BEWARE
HIGH VOLTAGE

High voltages can cause damage and even death to people. Fortunately, the signals from your brain are very, very low voltage.

Nervous system signal	0.1 volts
Small flashlight battery	1.5 volts
Car battery	12 volts
Electric eel shock	600 volts
Electric fence shock	3,000 volts

This table lists some shocking voltages!

Nerve Centers

Different parts of the brain are "wired" to different parts of the body. This means that nerves from certain parts of the body send signals to certain parts of the brain. There are lots of **nerve centers** in the brain. These deal with separate things such as touch, taste, movement, and speech.

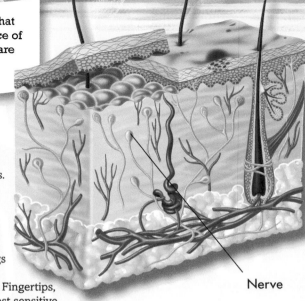

This diagram shows what lies beneath the surface of your skin. The nerves are shown in blue.

Touch Center

You use your skin to touch things. Touch is one of the body's senses. Nerves in your skin detect different things, such as heat, cold, pain, light touch, and heavy pressure. Some parts have more nerve endings than others, and so are more sensitive to touch. Fingertips, lips, and toes are the most sensitive.

Nerve

Under Pressure

The air all around you is constantly putting pressure on your skin. Atmospheric pressure at sea level is 14.2 pounds per square inch (1 kilogram per square centimeter)—this is known as one bar of pressure. If you dive 33 feet (10 meters) underwater, the pressure is 2 bar, or 28.4 pounds per square inch (2 kilograms per square centimeter). You would feel this water pressing on your skin. In space, there is no air, so no air pressure. That's why astronauts wear spacesuits outside their spacecraft. The suits are filled with pressurized air.

Nourish Your Brain

Your brain needs energy and **nutrients** from the food that you eat. It gets these through your blood. **Blood vessels** run up your neck and all around your brain. Blood also supplies your brain with oxygen. Your brain is greedy—although it is only about 2 percent of your body weight, it needs 15–20 percent of your body's blood supply!

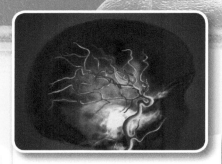

This image shows some of the blood vessels in the brain.

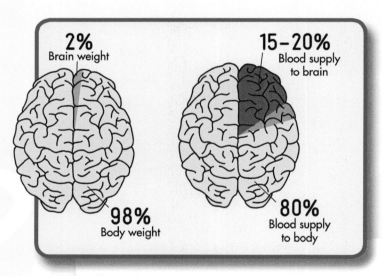

2%
Brain weight

15–20%
Blood supply to brain

98%
Body weight

80%
Blood supply to body

These charts show the **proportion** of body weight that the brain makes up, and the much larger proportion of blood that your brain needs.

Blood is also responsible for removing things that your brain doesn't need, such as carbon dioxide. This poisonous gas is made when your cells use oxygen to release energy from your food. In addition to this, blood carries some chemicals that are made in your brain to the parts of your body that need them.

Babies that are cuddled and talked to will have more developed brains than neglected babies, who have the same number of neurons but fewer connections.

The Growing Brain

The brain of a new baby gets about three times bigger in its first year. Some of this growth takes place because of the energy and nutrients from the baby's food. But the brain also grows as a result of the baby's experiences—seeing, hearing, feeling, touching, and tasting things. These all strengthen the connections between the neurons.

Teenage Brains

Human brains go through a huge "rewiring" process during the teenage years. Some connections in the brain speed up and get stronger. Others—the ones that are not used as much—shrink or get cut. This "rewiring" process might help to explain some teenage behaviors, such as mood swings.

Making Sense of It All

Your body can sense touch, and it has four other senses. These are sight, smell, taste, and hearing. They can all detect changes in your surroundings, and they feed messages to your brain. Your brain can then decide what to do with the information, and it can react to keep you safe.

Many birds have excellent eyesight. Sparrows have twice the **concentration** of cells on the retina that humans have; buzzards have five times as much!

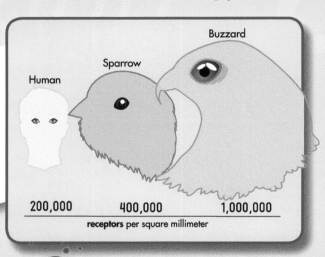

Human

Sparrow

Buzzard

200,000   400,000   1,000,000

receptors per square millimeter

Eye See

Your eyes collect light and send signals to your brain. Light passes through a clear pad called the lens at the front of the eye. Then it goes through a little black hole in the center called the pupil. The light ends up on the back wall of the eyeball, called the retina. From here, the optic nerve takes the signals to your brain.

Lenses Everywhere

You have one lens in each eye. Honeybee eyes have over 5,000, and dragonfly eyes have 30,000! Lots of insects have these **compound eyes**. They see the world quite differently from the way we see it.

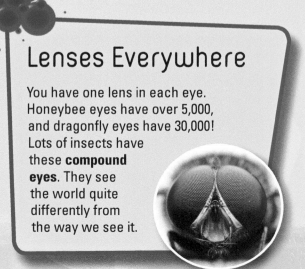

Do Your Eyes Deceive You?

Sometimes your brain can be tricked when you look at things. It fills in blanks to "see" things that aren't actually there, or it skips over things it doesn't need to see. It can also be persuaded to think something that isn't quite true, because of other factors that affect what you are looking at.

Giant Eye

Giant squid have huge eyes—over 10 inches (25 centimeters) in **diameter**! This is 10 times bigger than human eyes, which are about 1 inch (2.5 centimeters) in diameter.

In this picture, the man looks much bigger than the woman. In reality, the shape of the room is distorted to create an optical illusion.

Hear Me Now

Hearing is the sense that detects sounds. Soundwaves arrive into your ear through the ear canal. They hit the eardrum, and this begins to vibrate. Three tiny little bones deep in your ear start moving. This makes the liquid inside the **cochlea** move.

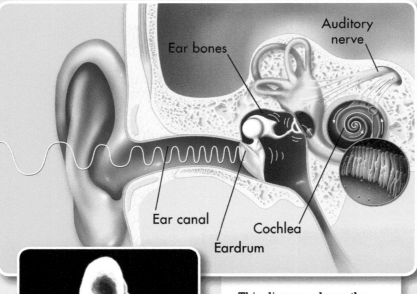

Auditory nerve

Ear bones

Ear canal

Cochlea

Eardrum

This diagram shows the path of sound in the ear.

Tiny hairs inside the cochlea trigger nerve cells. These send signals to your brain along the auditory nerve, and you hear the sound in your brain. The bendable part of your ear, on the outside of your head, traps and funnels soundwaves into your ear canal.

The three ear bones are the smallest in the body. One of them, the stirrup, is only 0.1 inch (2.5 millimeters) long.

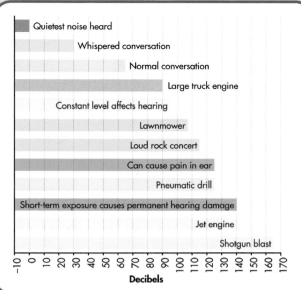

| | Quietest noise heard |
| Whispered conversation |
| Normal conversation |
| Large truck engine |
| Constant level affects hearing |
| Lawnmower |
| Loud rock concert |
| Can cause pain in ear |
| Pneumatic drill |
| Short-term exposure causes permanent hearing damage |
| Jet engine |
| Shotgun blast |

-10 0 10 20 30 40 50 60 70 80 90 100 110 120 130 140 150 160 170

Decibels

This bar chart shows the decibel levels of various sounds. You can see the sounds that may cause permanent damage to your hearing.

Pardon?

Loud sounds make big soundwaves, and quiet sounds make small soundwaves. High-pitched sounds make fast soundwaves, and low-pitched sounds make slow soundwaves. The nerve cells in your ears react differently to different sound levels and pitches.

Sound levels are measured in units called decibels (dB). The decibel scale starts from below zero, like the temperature scale. Some people can hear sounds as low as 0 dB. Sounds above about 85 dB can damage your hearing.

Who Said That?

You can tell where soundwaves are coming from because you have an ear on each side of your head. Soundwaves travel at about 1,082 feet (330 meters) per second. They hit the right or left ear fractionally before the other, so your brain can figure out where they come from.

Sniffing It Out

Smell is another of your senses. Smells are carried as tiny particles in the air and are breathed in through your nose. The particles hit millions of tiny hairs called cilia inside your nose. These are connected to nerve cells. They can detect 10,000 different smells, and they send signals to the smell center in your brain.

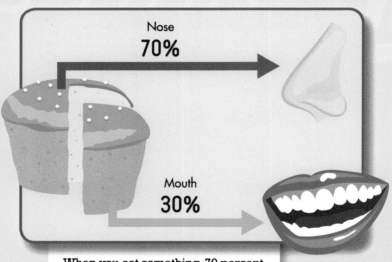

Nose
70%

Mouth
30%

When you eat something, 70 percent of the "taste" is actually detected by your nose, as a smell.

That Reminds Me...

The area of your brain that receives smell messages from your nose also deals with feelings, emotions, and memories. This is why some smells remind you of certain events or places, or bring back particular feelings.

Nosy Animals

The human sense of smell is not great compared to that of some animals. Dogs can smell at least 10,000 times better than us, which means that they can detect smells that we never could. The area of a dog's brain that is devoted to smell is much bigger than ours. If you calculated the ratio of smell center to brain size, a dog's would be 40 times larger than a human's. Dogs' superior sense of smell means they can work as rescue dogs, sniffing out people buried after avalanches or earthquakes.

Sharks have an excellent sense of smell—they can detect a drop of blood in the ocean from $1/4$ mile (400 meters) away!

Life Without Smells

Some people have a condition called anosmia, which means they cannot smell anything. Sometimes this is caused by the nose being blocked, such as when you have a bad cold. Sometimes people damage the part of the brain that deals with smells, and so even though the particles of smell trigger the nerve cells in the nose, the message does not reach the brain.

Tastes Great!

You use your mouth—especially your tongue—for your sense of taste.
Your tongue has about 10,000 little taste buds on it. Each taste bud has
50–100 nerve cells, with a tiny hair sticking out of each one. All the tastes
that wash over your tongue are detected by these hairs. The nerve cells at
the end of the hairs send messages to the taste center in your brain.

Tongue Twisters

Can you touch your nose with your
tongue? A nectar bat can stick out
its tongue so it is 1½ times as long
as its body! These bats eat nectar
from a long, tube-shaped flower.
Chameleons' tongues are also 1½
times as long as their bodies. They
shoot out their tongues to catch
flying insects.

Taste Buds

Taste buds can detect five
different basic tastes in food.
These are sweet, salty, sour,
bitter, and umami. Umami is
a savory taste that was not
generally known about until
the 1980s.

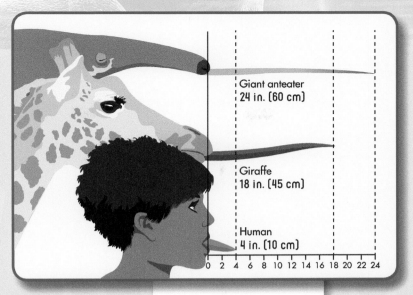

Giant anteater
24 in. (60 cm)

Giraffe
18 in. (45 cm)

Human
4 in. (10 cm)

0 2 4 6 8 10 12 14 16 18 20 22 24

Some animals have
really long tongues!

Hot, Hot, Hot!

When you eat spicy food such as chilis, it is not your tongue's taste senses
that are being stimulated, but its pain sensors. When you eat a chili, it feels like
your tongue is on fire. This is because your brain sends the same response as
it would if your tongue really was on fire! Scientists think this may be why we
enjoy eating chilis—we get a strong reaction, but we know there is no harm
being done. We just like the thrill!

The hotness
of peppers is
measured using
something called
the Scoville
scale. It ranges
from 0 (yellow
bell pepper) to
16 million (pure
capsaicin, the
chemical that
makes the heat).

Are You in Control?

You take control over lots of things that your body does. You decide to walk, type, think, jump, read, chew, and do a thousand other things. But your brain also carries out many tasks automatically, without you even realizing.

Control Your Actions

When you decide to move, the thought starts in the motor area of your brain, in the cerebral cortex. Electrical signals are sent along nerves that deal with muscles and movement, called motor nerves. They go to the part of your body that you want to move, and the signals tell the muscles there to get moving.

Supersonic Bite

Trap-jaw ants have the fastest bite on the planet. They can bite down on their prey, moving their jaws at an amazing 146 miles (235 kilometers) per hour! That's 2,300 times faster than you can blink your eyelid.

Control Your Reactions

Your reaction time is the time that elapses between your brain thinking about moving and the correct part of your body actually moving. Consider athletes lined up at the start of a 100-meter race. They are all ready to go when they hear the starter gun. They need to develop really quick reaction times to get up and running as soon as the gun goes off.

You and your friends can test your reaction times. Hold a 12-inch (30-centimeter) ruler upright between your thumb and forefinger (hold the ruler right at the bottom end). Now let go, and catch it again immediately. How far up the ruler did your fingers close on it again? Which of your friends has the quickest reaction time?

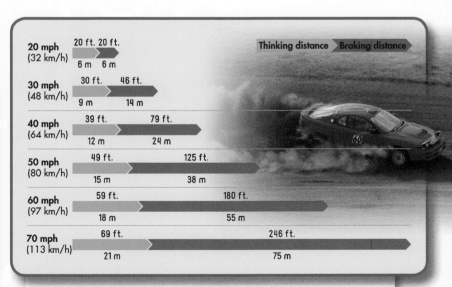

	Thinking distance	Braking distance
20 mph (32 km/h)	20 ft. / 6 m	20 ft. / 6 m
30 mph (48 km/h)	30 ft. / 9 m	46 ft. / 14 m
40 mph (64 km/h)	39 ft. / 12 m	79 ft. / 24 m
50 mph (80 km/h)	49 ft. / 15 m	125 ft. / 38 m
60 mph (97 km/h)	59 ft. / 18 m	180 ft. / 55 m
70 mph (113 km/h)	69 ft. / 21 m	246 ft. / 75 m

This graph shows how far cars travel before stopping when they are moving at certain speeds. The blue part of each bar shows the distance the car covers while the driver reacts to the situation. The red part of each bar shows the distance covered while the car slows down and stops.

No Control

Your brain runs certain things in your body without you even realizing that some of them need to be run at all! These are all automatic actions, and you have little or no control over when they happen. Breathing is one of these automatic actions. You breathe all day and all night without thinking about it. You take around 12–20 breaths every minute when you are at rest, and more if you are moving around or exercising.

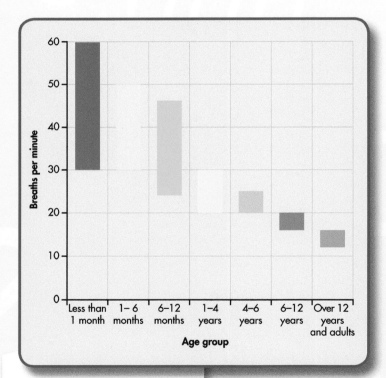

This bar chart shows the range of normal breathing rates (breaths per minute) for babies, children, and adults. Breathing rates generally slow down through childhood.

Any kind of exercise causes your heart rate to increase.

Your Beating Heart

Much of this automatic control is carried out by the brain stem. It controls your heartbeat. At rest, the average adult heart beats between 60 and 100 times per minute. The heart rate of a mouse is about 500 beats per minute. An elephant's heart beats around 28 times per minute. When you exercise, your body needs more blood to be pumped around it, to carry more oxygen to your muscles. This is why your heart rate goes up.

Deep Breaths

An average adult's lungs can draw in about 12.7 pints (6 liters) of air. Enormous blue whales have a **lung capacity** of about 1,300 gallons (5,000 liters)! They dive for around 20 minutes at a time, so they need to take a huge, deep breath of oxygen before they go underwater.

Inner Workings

All the food you eat has to be processed by your body. This is called digestion, and it is controlled by your brain. All you have to do is put the food in your mouth, chew, and swallow! Your brain and your digestive system take care of the rest. They also get rid of your body's waste products—**feces** and **urine**. All you need to do is...go to the bathroom.

Your brain also tells your skin to sweat when you are hot, and it controls other liquids such as tears and saliva. Your mouth produces over 2 pints (1 liter) of saliva every day—enough to fill between four and eight glasses! The blood flowing around your body is controlled by your brain, too. It automatically decides when and where to send the blood, depending on which parts of your body need it most.

Your brain controls bodily fluids such as tears, saliva, and urine.

When you taste something sour, such as lemon juice, your taste buds are stimulated and you start producing more saliva.

Reflex Action

Sometimes your body needs to react quickly to something, without you having to think about it and control it. Your nervous system has **reflexes** to do this. These are simple actions that you sometimes can't control—such as coughing, blinking, swallowing, or removing your hand from something really hot. The messages to do these actions don't actually come from your brain, though. They come straight from your spinal cord. This means that the action can be done really quickly, to help keep you safe.

Animal Actions

Animals have reflexes, too. Larger animals have much slower reflex times than smaller ones. A test comparing elephants and shrews found that the shrews' response times were 100 times faster than the elephants'. This is simply because the messages had to travel farther in the elephants.

Your Amazing Brain

Your brain does much more than move your body and keep your insides working properly. It is where you store memories and learn things. It is where your feelings and emotions come from. It can also make chemicals that affect both the brain and the body. Your brain is a busy organ that needs to rest while you sleep in order to be able to perform all these functions properly.

Lifelong Learning

From the minute you are born, you start learning things. Learning includes repeating an experience until it sticks in your head. Small babies learn what their parents look, sound, and smell like. You learn how to read and write, you learn facts about things, and you learn how to apply information to different situations.

All in Your Mind

When you think about something, your brain can recall what it has already learned about it. For example, if you think about thunder and lightning, you can "picture" the lightning in your head and "hear" the rumbling noise.

Age	Number of words a child can say
1	20
2	200–300
3	900–1,000
4	1,500–1,600
5	2,100–2,200
6	2,600 (but can understand 20,000–24,000)
12	Can understand 50,000, can say most of them

You start learning how to say new words when you are around one year old. You will probably keep learning new words all your life!

Everyone Can Learn!

You have around 100 billion brain cells. The tiny vinegar worm has only 302! Even so, it can learn. It learns not to eat a certain kind of **bacteria** that makes it sick.

A clever computer might be able to recognize your face, but it would not be able to tell from your face if you were happy, sad, excited, or bored. Computers cannot learn and adapt like human brains can, and they don't have feelings and emotions. So never think your computer is smarter than you!

Remember When...

Think back to an event you enjoyed, such as a vacation. Where did you go? What was the weather like? The more you think about it, the more you can remember. You can start to remember not only sights and scenes, but also how something tasted or smelled or made you feel. Can you remember how you were feeling at the time?

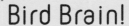

Bird Brain!

Pigeons have excellent memories. Scientists have tested their memories using pictures of different things. When the pigeons were shown a picture, they remembered to peck in a certain place. They managed to remember 800–1,200 pictures. One bird could remember 68 percent of 1,978 pictures—that's 1,345 pictures!

Average age people experience memory loss	57 years
Age at which memory loss can begin	30 years
People in a survey noticing memory loss in their thirties	6%
People in a survey noticing memory loss in their forties	11%
People in a survey worried about losing keys	19%
People in a survey worried about forgetting people's names	37%

As you age, you can start to lose your memory! So make sure you keep it sharp by trying to remember all sorts of things.

Scientists think that a memory is made up of a set of links between brain cells. These links travel along a certain pathway in your brain. Every time you think about a past event, the links fire along the same pathway. The pathways get stronger the more you use them, so the more you think about something, the more powerfully you will remember it.

The Long and the Short of It

There are two types of memory—short-term and long-term. Short-term memory holds information for only a few minutes, such as the color of the car that just drove past. It can hold some information for up to a few days, such as what you had for lunch during the weekend. But your brain does not need to remember unimportant things like this, so after a while, the memory is lost.

Long-term memories can remain for years. Things such as how to ride a bike, knowing people's names and faces, and recognizing the names of animals and objects are long-term memories.

Knowing how to ride a bike is stored in your long-term memory—it's something you're not likely to forget!

Chemical Control

Your brain needs help from chemicals called **hormones** to keep everything running smoothly. Some hormones are made in the brain, while others are made elsewhere in your body. One of the hormones made in the brain is growth hormone. This controls the rate at which you grow, and it is mainly produced while you are asleep. Some children have conditions that affect the part of the brain that produces the growth hormone, and they stop growing as they should.

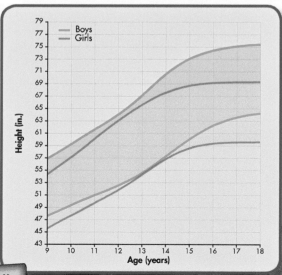

This graph shows the normal growth curves for boys and girls between the ages of 9 and 18. There is a wide range of normal heights. Children below the normal ranges may have less growth hormone than usual.

Fight or Flight?

Adrenaline is a hormone that your body produces when you are frightened. It is made in your adrenal glands, which are near the kidneys, in your lower back. Adrenaline goes all around your body, including to your brain, and affects lots of things:

- Your heart beats faster.
- Your lungs breathe deeper and faster.
- More blood goes to your muscles.
- Less blood goes to parts that don't need it, such as your skin.
- Your pupils open wide.
- Your skin sweats.
- Your brain goes on high alert.

All of these things make your body ready to run away from the thing that scared you...or stay put and fight it!

Stressful Training

Many soldiers have to go through very stressful training programs to make sure they can cope with real-life situations. One such program is called Survival, Evasion, Resistance, Escape (SERE). Some soldiers have had the adrenaline levels in their blood measured before, during, and after SERE training. Before and after training, the levels were around 25 nanograms per milliliter. During training, the levels shot up to 150 nanograms per milliliter!

Recharging the Brain

You sleep for about one-third of your life! Your brain doesn't switch off while you sleep, though. It still has lots of vital things to run in your body, and many signals moving all around it. Scientists think that while you sleep, your brain is busy filtering through the information and memories of that day, sorting it all into the right places.

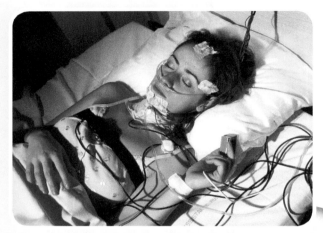

Scientists can measure the activity of the brain while people are asleep. They tape wires to the head that can pick up electrical activity in the brain. They use these to see people's sleep patterns.

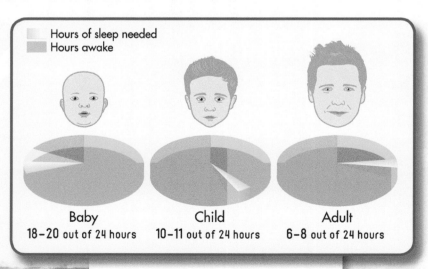

Hours of sleep needed
Hours awake

Baby	Child	Adult
18–20 out of 24 hours	10–11 out of 24 hours	6–8 out of 24 hours

We need different amounts of sleep at different times of our lives.

Sleep Stages

You go through different stages of sleep throughout the night. Your sleep varies between times of deep sleep (when you don't dream) and lighter sleep (when you do dream). But at all times, you can wake suddenly—if you hear a loud noise or someone shakes you awake, for example.

Amount of time you spend sleeping over a year	122 days
Amount of time you spend sleeping over a lifetime (75 years)	25 years
Average number of times in a night when you might dream	5
Percentage of people who dream in black and white	12%
Amount of time it takes after waking to forget 90% of your dreams	10 minutes
Longest recorded time a person has gone without sleep	18 days, 21 hours, 40 minutes

Sleepy Animals

Do you think you sleep a lot? Brown bats sleep for about 20 hours a day. Lions sleep for around 14 hours. Animals that eat grass and leaves have to spend a long time grazing, so they sleep less. Horses sleep around three hours a day, and giraffes for only two hours. Dolphins can only let one half of their brains sleep at a time, because they need their brains to make sure they don't drown!

Just like any other part of the body, brains can get injured or be affected by diseases. The brain itself has no pain receptors, so it does not feel sore, but a sick or injured brain can affect the rest of the body.

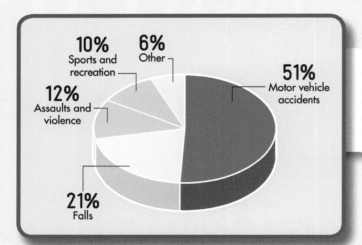

10% Sports and recreation

6% Other

51% Motor vehicle accidents

12% Assaults and violence

21% Falls

This pie chart shows the causes of brain injuries.

Brain Injury

Brains can be injured in accidents, such as car crashes. If part of the brain is damaged, the function of that part is affected. For example, a person may lose the ability to move part of his or her body, speak, learn, remember, or concentrate, depending on the part of the brain that is hurt. If the brain stem is damaged, the person may lose the automatic control of his or her breathing or heart rate.

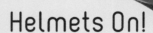

Helmets On!

Do you have a bicycle? Do you go out on the roads? Did you know that about 75 percent of cyclists killed in a traffic accident die of a head injury? Did you also know that 85 percent of bicycle accident head injuries can be prevented by wearing a helmet?

Percentage of people having a mental illness at some point	25%
Percentage of children with a mental illness at a given time	10%
Percentage of older people affected by depression	20%
Percentage of people in prison with some kind of mental illness	90%

Mental Illnesses

Sometimes people can have mental illnesses, like depression or anxiety. These illnesses can be caused by lots of things. Stress, social problems, and chemical imbalances are some of the causes. Mental illnesses can affect how people think, feel, and behave. They can be treated in different ways.

Depression is a very common mental illness. It can cause people to have low moods, lose interest in things, feel guilty and worthless, have trouble sleeping, have little energy, and be unable to concentrate.

Aging Brains

As brains get older, they can be affected by **dementia** and can stop working as they should. Lots of things cause dementia, including Alzheimer's disease, which makes the brain shrink. Dementia makes brain cells become damaged, and connections between cells get broken. It can affect things such as memory, thinking speed, mental agility, language, understanding, and judgment.

Alzheimer's

Over five million people in the United States have Alzheimer's disease, and around 800,000 of them live alone. The disease is the sixth leading cause of death.

Keeping fit and eating a healthy diet can help to lower the risk of developing dementia.

Meningitis

Meningitis is a disease that causes the thin layers between the brain and the skull—the meninges—to get infected and swell up. This puts pressure on the brain. It can cause severe headaches, vomiting, fever, a stiff neck, and a skin rash. There are two main types of meningitis—bacterial (caused by bacteria) and viral (caused by a **virus**).

If it isn't treated, bacterial meningitis can result in severe brain damage. The bacteria can get into the blood and cause blood poisoning. If this happens, the poisoned blood can affect other parts of the body, such as the hands, arms, feet, and legs. People may have to have these parts amputated and in the worst cases, they may even die.

Average number of cases of meningitis per year in the United States (1998 to 2007)	1,500
Percentage of people in the United States with meningitis who die as a result	11%
Percentage of people in the United States with meningitis who suffer long-term damage (e.g., brain damage, kidney disease, hearing loss)	20%
Time after contracting meningitis that some people can die	4 hours
Number of deaths around the world every year from bacterial meningitis	170,000

Epilepsy

Here are some statistics about meningitis in the United States and around the world.

Some people have epilepsy. This causes sudden bursts of electrical energy in parts of the brain. These can disrupt the normal electrical messages. Epilepsy can cause people to have seizures. These can be very small, but some seizures can be much more severe, causing the whole body to stiffen and jerk.

Think of a Number

You only have one brain—but one brain is all you need to run things in your body for your whole life.

Remember, your one amazing brain:

- has about 100 billion brain cells and is 75 percent water
- stores about 100,000 gigabytes worth of memories
- uses 20 percent of your energy
- is connected to around 93,000 miles (150,000 kilometers) of nerves in your body
- sends messages around your body at up to 270 miles (435 kilometers) per hour
- sees, hears, smells, tastes, and feels for you
- keeps your heart pumping and your lungs breathing
- rests while you sleep.

Your brain is amazing. It can run lots of things for you simultaneously, while you get on with your life!

You Can Help It!

You need to ensure you take care of your all-important brain. Make sure you give it enough rest by getting a good night's sleep every night. Be sure to drink enough water—remember, three-quarters of your brain is water! Also make sure you feed it well. Eat healthy food full of vitamins and minerals. Your digestive system will get to work on the food to send good stuff to your brain.

It is also important to keep your brain safe from harm. Protect it when you are out cycling, skateboarding, skiing, snowboarding, inline skating, or doing anything else that involves speed or heights. Be sure to wear a helmet that fits your head properly. This will help to protect your precious brain if you fall.

You should also exercise your brain! Keep it active by learning new things and doing new activities. Keep precious memories alive by bringing them to mind once in a while.

Test Yourself!

Take a look at the questions below. You will find all the answers somewhere in this book. Check out the pages where the information is if you need reminding of the answers.

1 Which nerve in your body is about as wide as your thumb?
a   the spinal cord
b   the sciatic nerve
c   the optic nerve

2 How many different smells can the nerve cells in your nose detect?
a   1,000
b   10,000
c   100,000

3 If your brain used up 450 calories of the energy you got from your food in one day, and you ate 2,250 calories that day, what percentage of your energy intake did your brain use up?
a   10%
b   15%
c   20%

4 Which nerve carries signals from your eyes to your brain?
a   auditory nerve
b   olfactory nerve
c   optic nerve

5 Approximately how much time do you spend asleep over the course of a year?
a   82 days
b   102 days
c   122 days

6 Match these animals to their resting heart rates:
animals: human; mouse; elephant
resting heart rates: 500; 28; 60

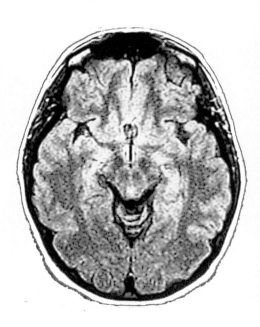

7 Approximately how much of your brain is water?

a   75%
b   55%
c   35%

8 What is umami?

a   a smell
b   a taste
c   a sound

9 How much air can an adult draw into his or her lungs when taking a deep breath?

a   12.7 pints (6 liters)
b   21 pints (10 liters)
c   30 pints (14 liters)

10 Which units are used to measure how loud something is?

a   soundwaves
b   pitches
c   decibels

Deep in the Brain

There is a part of your brain, in the diencephalon, that is about the size of a grape. It lies just below another part, called the thalamus. It controls lots of your feelings, such as anger and happiness. It sends signals to the pituitary gland, telling it when to release its hormones. Can you do some research and try to find out the name of this important part of your brain?

Answers:
1b; 2b; 3c; 4c; 5c; 6: human = 60, mouse = 500, elephant = 28; 7a; 8b; 9a; 10c

Glossary

axon long part of a nerve cell that sends out nerve messages

bacteria tiny living things that you can't see but that live on and in your body

blood vessel any of the tubes in the body that blood flows through

cerebral cortex folded outer layer of the brain

circumference distance all the way around something

cochlea part of the inner ear, shaped like a snail shell, that creates nerve messages

compound eye eye with lots of lenses, such as many insects have

concentration amount of a certain substance that there is in another substance

dementia mental illness caused by illness or injury in the brain

dendrite part of a nerve cell that receives nerve messages

diameter distance from one side of an object to the other, passing through its central point

feces solid waste that passes out of the body through the anus

frequency how often something takes place

hormone chemical made in the body; hormones move around in the blood and affect certain organs

lung capacity amount of air your lungs can hold when full

nerve fiber in the body made of nerve cells that carries messages to and from the brain and other parts of the body

nerve center group of nerve cells in the brain that are responsible for performing a particular function in the body

nervous system network of nerve cells that connects your body parts to your brain

neuron special cell that sends nerve messages around your body

nutrient something that a living thing needs in order to grow and survive

organ part of your body that performs a particular task, such as the heart or lungs

proportion amount of something, compared to something else

ratio figure describing how big something is, or how much there is, in relation to something else

receptor nerve ending that sends sensory messages to the brain

reflex action that your body does automatically, without you thinking about or controlling it, such as sneezing or coughing

sciatic nerve large nerve at the bottom of the spinal cord, extending down the thigh

urine liquid waste that passes out of the body through the urethra

virus tiny things that can enter your body and cause illness and disease

Find Out More

BOOKS

Parker, Steve. *Brain* (Body Focus). Chicago: Heinemann Library, 2010.

Riley, Joelle. *Your Nervous System* (Searchlight Books: How Does Your Body Work?). Minneapolis: Lerner Classroom, 2012.

Seuling, Barbara. *Your Skin Weighs More Than Your Brain and Other Freaky Facts About Your Skin, Skeleton, and Other Body Parts* (Freaky Facts). Mankato, Minn.: Capstone, 2008.

Walker, Richard. *Human Body* (Eyewitness). New York: Dorling Kindersley, 2012.

WEB SITES
faculty.washington.edu/chudler/introb.html
This web site has lots of really interesting, strange, and amazing information about the brain and nervous system.

kidshealth.org/kid/htbw/brain.html
Here you can find out lots of information about the brain and nervous system, and there are diagrams to click on and find out more.

kids.nationalgeographic.com/kids/stories/spacescience/brain
On this National Geographic web site, you can find out all about your amazing brain.

FURTHER RESEARCH
You could visit your local library to see if there are any books on the brain and the nervous system. You could also do some research to find out how people are affected by brain injuries or by spinal cord injuries. Some people manage to overcome really serious injuries where they have to re-learn how to do very basic things.

Index